SAILOR MOON ®

Sailor Moon® the novel #4

MARS ATTACKS

**Written by
Lianne Sentar**

**Created by
NAOKO TAKEUCHI**

=) SMILE books

Published by Mixx Entertainment, Inc.
Los Angeles • Tokyo
www.mixxonline.com

RL 4, 008-012

Mixx Entertainment presents
Sailor Moon the novel #4 • *Mars Attacks*
Published on the SMILE Books imprint
ISBN: 1-892213-27-3

Printed in the United States

First printing January 2000

10 9 8 7 6 5 4 3 2 1

Chapter 1
It's All in
the Charm

The sun shone brightly on Crossroads. Birds chirped; squirrels frolicked; everyone was enjoying the day—except for the group of teenage girls gathered around the 666 bus stop. They weren't like ordinary teenagers. None of them laughed or chatted. They just stood, staring blankly ahead, as they waited for the 666 bus.

The girls held small charms, pieces of parchment mounted on boards of red and gold. Charms for good luck were written on the parchment in thick black ink.

The 666 bus approached and slid to a stop in

front of the group. The door barely whispered as it unfolded, letting the zombified girls trudge aboard. The bus driver's sharply angled face was barely visible behind a low-brimmed hat. She snarled as the last girl found a seat.

As the bus pulled away, the air in front of it began to ripple. A vortex formed high in the sky— a portal to another dimension. The driver tilted the steering wheel up. The bus lifted off the ground, flew toward the portal, and disappeared into the vortex. Once the vehicle had passed through, the vortex grew smaller, until it, too, had disappeared from the sky. All that remained was a single good luck charm, resting on the sidewalk by the 666 bus stop.

"You fiend!" Serena Tsukino tossed back her long blond hair, and clenched her fists for dramatic effect. "Give those girls back! I protect this city from scum like you, and in the name of all that is good, you're punished!"

Amy Anderson, Serena's friend, looked up from the Calculus book she was studying. "What did you just say, Serena?"

mars attacks

Serena jumped down from the park bench she had been perched on. She grinned and held up a comic book for Amy to see.

"In the new issue of Sailor V," Serena said breathlessly, "a bunch of girls get trapped in a building by some evil guy, and Sailor V has to save them. Sailor V's dialogue is so great, I just have to read it out loud. With all the theatrics, of course."

Serena jumped back onto the bench, struck a fighter's pose, and shouted: "I, Sailor V, will defeat you with one blow!"

Amy went back to her Calculus. "I do believe you're the only person I know who can turn motionless picture entertainment into an interactive experience, Serena."

Serena smiled. Maybe she did have a flair for the dramatic, perhaps even the over-dramatic. But being chic teenager by day, Champion of Justice, Sailor Moon by night was demanding work. What was wrong, Serena asked herself, with having a little fun?

Serena hugged the comic to her chest. Nothing made her as happy as a brand-new Sailor V graphic novel. Life was good.

"This has been such a great day, Ames," Serena declared. She spun around, and nearly toppled off the bench.

"Maybe you should follow Amy's lead," remarked Luna, Serena's sometimes-annoying talking cat. The feline, curled by Amy's feet, cocked an eyebrow. "Since you have no homework, Serena, now would be the perfect time to catch up on all the classes you're so hideously behind in."

Serena rolled her eyes. "As if, Luna." Serena hated studying when she had to—there was no way she was going to do it on her day off.

"Speaking of classes," Amy said, not looking up, "how are you doing in science, Serena? Our test's coming up soon. Need help studying?"

"Stop thinking about school for once," Serena said with a frown. "You're gonna have a melt-down if you don't relax a little more, Ames. Wanna get some ice cream? I'm getting a major chocolate craving."

Amy licked her index finger and turned a page of her Calculus book. "Better go on without me." Amy brushed back a strand of her stylishly short blue hair. "This book is so fascinating."

Serena shivered. Amy actually liked school. They had been friends for a while now—ever since Serena had discovered the genius Amy was fellow Sailor Scout Mercury—but Serena was still having trouble accepting Amy's warped conception of fun. Serena shook her head. The blue-haired girl had once actually said she preferred the Learning Channel to MTV.

"Come on, Amy," Serena said exasperatedly, pulling at the thin girl's arm. "Ditch the math and get some Rocky Road with me. I don't wanna go by myself—pigging out's no fun if you're alone."

"Pigging out's no fun, period," Amy answered. "Stuffing yourself isn't healthy."

"Not healthy?! Sugar is brain food!"

"Actually," Amy replied, "scientifically speaking, it's not the sugar, it's the glucose—"

Amy stopped talking as two visibly upset women passed by, talking quickly.

"Did you hear?" one of the women asked, shaking her head. "The 666 bus vanished yesterday afternoon. They say as many as fifty teenage girls were on it."

Serena, Amy, and Luna all froze.

"Vanished?" The second woman frowned. "You mean, they have no idea where it went?"

"No idea at all. It's as if it disappeared into thin air."

The second woman clutched her chest. "Goodness. I hope they find them. My daughter's a teenager, and if she vanished like that, I don't know what I'd do."

"I know. Think of all those girls' parents. They must be out of their minds with worry."

As the women walked away, Serena felt a little shiver down her spine. An entire bus had vanished into thin air? How could that happen? Serena gasped suddenly. Oh no, she thought, it couldn't be...

"The Enemy!" Luna jumped onto the bench and turned to the two girls. "Did you hear those women? If what they said was true, I'd bet the Enemy is behind it! It's just their style, kidnapping people for their energy!"

"Right." Amy nodded quickly and shoved her book aside. "Buses don't vanish into thin air. It's got to be the work of the Enemy."

mars attacks

With a groan, Serena buried her face in her hands. Great. Those stupid bad guys were at it again. Couldn't they find other ways to spend their time besides sucking the energy from innocent victims in Crossroads? Demon golf, perhaps?

There went her afternoon plans, Serena thought. It was only a matter of time, she knew, before she heard that dirty little eleven-letter word. I-N-V-E-S-T-I-G-A-T-E.

"Serena," Luna said firmly, "I think you should investigate."

Serena rolled her eyes—right on cue.

"We'll split up," Amy declared, standing up. "I'll check the news reports for today. Maybe they'll have more information."

Serena crossed her arms in frustration. This superhero business could be so aggravating. Now she couldn't get her chocolate hit. And the day had started out so well.

"The 666 bus." Amy stroked her chin in thought. "That stop's not far from here. It's right near the sacred Shinto temple on Cherry Hill, if I'm not mistaken. Serena, why don't you check out the temple? It might have something to do with the

7

bus' disappearance."

Serena let out a long, loud sigh. "Do I really have to?" she complained. "I was looking forward to taking a humongous nap this afternoon."

"Serena!" Luna snapped. "Cut it out. This isn't a shopping trip, it's Sailor business." The cat crossed her arms. "You can't expect everything to be fun and games. This is your duty."

"Serena," Amy said, a twinkle in her eye." You know, the temple sells love charms, don't you? Maybe you could get one while you're there."

Serena blinked. Love charms? She imagined herself with one of those charms in her pocket, walking into the Crown Arcade where that hottie Andrew Foreman worked. He would just have to fall instantly in love with her.

"All right!" Serena cried, clapping her hands. "Hey, maybe this won't be such a bummer after all!" Andrew was such a babe.

Luna stomped on Serena's foot to get her attention. "Serena," the cat said lowly, "don't get carried away. This is an investi--"

"Yeah, yeah," Serena muttered as she brushed Luna off. "Whatever."

She rubbed her hands together and smiled. "A love charm. Too cool!"

Luna's eyes narrowed. "Sere--"

Serena clapped a hand over Luna's mouth and pulled the cat into her arms. "Great," Serena declared as Luna struggled to get free. "I'm outta here. Catch you later, Ames."

The blue-haired girl shook her head as she watched Serena skip down the street.

"The things Serena will do for love," she muttered as she picked up her Calculus book and slipped it into her book bag. "She can be so predictable."

Amy began walking in the direction of Crossroads News Station. She laughed to herself. "I suppose I should just be happy the temple doesn't feature an all-you-can-eat buffet."

At the Cherry Hill temple, a tall blond man in a Shinto priest's outfit quietly swept the stone floor. Behind him, three girls ran up the long flight of steps squealing excitedly.

"This is so cool!" one of them cried. "Once I get that love charm, I'm sure Bobby will fall in love with me!"

"And Mike will probably beg to drive me to school every day," another girl said with a giggle. "He's so cute."

As the girls skipped into the temple, the blond priest smiled. "Ah," he said under his breath, "to be young and in love."

The man looked up. His cold blue eyes glinted as they caught the sunlight. "Such passion, such energy," Jedite whispered with a chuckle. "The Negaverse will have your energy soon enough."

Chapter 2
Temple Trouble

Serena reached the Cherry Hill Temple quickly. She had always been a fast runner—she was practically Olympic-caliber thanks to all her practice racing to school each morning—but this time she almost flew. All she could think about was how great it would be to have Andrew on his knees proposing to her.

Cool, Serena thought, as she raced up the temple stairs. Andrew was finally going to go gaga over her. It was about time. How he had managed to overlook her beauty and charm for this long, she had no idea. "Hmm," she said to herself, "I wonder what color I should have my bridesmaids wear?"

"Serena!" cried a familiar voice from behind.

Serena stopped and turned around. Her face lit up when she saw her friends Molly Baker and Lisa Brownridge running up the gray stone steps. Luna squirmed out of Serena's grasp and scrambled onto her shoulder.

"Guys!" Serena shouted. She raced to them and gave them quick hugs. "What are you doing here?"

Lisa blushed. "We heard about the love charms," she said with a giggle. "We wanted to come get some and see if they really work."

Serena smirked as they walked up the stairs and made their way into the temple. "I guess great minds really do think alike," she commented. "I'm here for a love charm, too."

Molly laughed. "Who is it this week?" she teased. "The guy behind the counter at Baskin Robbins, or the Pizza Hut deliver boy."

Serena rolled her eyes. "Ha, ha."

A short old man suddenly popped out of nowhere. He was bald, and wore a Shinto priest's outfit: a long, white blouse, and baggy, light blue pants. His face lit up from ear to ear with a huge smile.

"Hello, girls!" he called cheerfully.

Serena stopped abruptly. Woah, she thought, as she looked him over. Who's this little guy? He looked like a miniature Mr. Clean, only not nearly as ripped.

"Do you work here?" Serena asked politely.

"I sure do!" he cried, clasping his hands behind his back. He grinned at Molly and Lisa. "My, you all seem like such nice kids. Wanna work for me?"

The three girls looked at each other.

"What?" Lisa asked, surprised. "Work here?"

The old man laughed and rocked back on his heels. "I'm always looking for help. So? What do you say?"

"Grandpa," barked a voice. "Are you bugging the visitors again?"

Serena looked up to see a dark haired teenage girl approaching. The girl wore an outfit similar to the old man's, except that her pants were red. The girl crossed her arms angrily.

The old man pouted. "Aw, Raye," he said. "I

was simply trying to get more helpers."

Raye was the prettiest girl Serena had ever seen. Her face was nearly flawless, with finely cut features, full lips and large eyes. Her hair was a silky midnight-black, and her dark eyes shimmered with a purple tint when the light caught them.

"Don't you ever quit?" she scolded. "We have enough workers, Grandpa. Please don't bother these girls. I'm sure they're not here to work."

Serena couldn't help but stare at Raye. The priestess was so pretty—she almost had a Catherine Zeta-Jones thing going.

As Raye took her grandfather's hand and led him away, the girls gathered together to gossip.

"Serena," Lisa whispered. "Isn't that girl gorgeous? I'd kill to have her hair!"

"I've heard about her," Molly said. "She's the mysterious priestess who can sense evil and see the future."

"Way cool!" Serena was impressed. "A mysterious priestess with the beauty of a goddess. It's like something out of a romance novel."

Luna jumped onto Serena's shoulder.

mars attacks

"Serena," the cat whispered angrily. "What are you doing? This isn't romantic at all. Fifty people are missing, and it might have something to do with this temple. Stay focused and start investigating."

Serena shook her head. Luna was always pulling Serena out of the clouds. Why couldn't that bossy cat just let Serena float there every once in a while?

On the far side of the temple, another group of schoolgirls walked down the temple stairs clutching the good luck charms they had just purchased. The blond man sweeping the stone floor looked up at them.

Jedite smiled. "Like taking candy from a baby," he whispered as he thrust out his hand.

Bolts of white light flashed from the good luck charms, striking each girl in the chest. The girls fell to the floor, unconscious, as the charms slowly drained the energy from their bodies.

Raye gasped. "I sense something." She let go of her grandfather and spun around.

"Evil," she cried, reaching into one of her wide sleeves. "I sense evil! No! I will not allow evil in this sacred place!" Raye whipped her head around and looked at Serena.

Serena's eyes went wide. "Huh?" she muttered. "Something wrong?"

Raye yanked out a piece of parchment with anti-evil symbols written on it and screamed: "Evil, be gone!"

With that, Raye leapt across the temple like a super ninja and slapped the parchment onto Serena's forehead. "I banish you! Be gone, evil spirit!"

Serena didn't have time to react. She collapsed to the floor like a ton of bricks. Molly gasped and dropped to her knees beside Serena.

"Serena!" she cried. "Oh my God!" Molly looked up at Raye with wild eyes. "What did you do?!"

Raye covered her mouth with her hand. "Oh, no!"

Raye's grandfather shook his head. "And you say I disrupt the visitors."

"Oh no," Raye whispered. She kneeled beside Serena. "It wasn't her. My sense was off. I'm so sorry!"

mars attacks

"Help me get her inside," Raye said as she struggled to lift Serena. "My God, this girl is heavy! What does she eat?"

"Whatever she can get her hands on," Molly replied, as she and Lisa helped Raye carry Serena inside the temple.

"Mmm." Drool trickled down Serena's chin. She rolled over on the cot. "Mmm, double-chocolate milkshake..."

"Serena," Luna whispered, nudging her Champion of Justice. "Serena, wake up."

Serena pushed Luna away and rolled over again. She giggled dreamily. "Yeah, Andrew," she murmured. "Hawaii'd be a great place for a honeymoon."

The paper-and-wood door slid open. Raye stepped into the room, followed by Molly and Lisa. Luna scurried away as Raye sat beside Serena. The priestess dipped a cloth into a bowl of cold water.

"She should be all right," Raye said quietly as she pressed the cloth to Serena's forehead. "She'll come around any minute."

Lisa gripped her knees and leaned forward.

"Raye," she said with a giggle. "That guy who gave you the water, the blond--what was his name?"

Molly blushed and smiled. "Yeah. He was really hot."

Serena's eyes shot wide open. She bolted from the cot. "Guy?" she screeched. "Blond? Hot? WHERE?"

Raye jumped back, spilling her bowl of water.

Molly laughed. "Woah," the red-head said with a whistle. "Serena, that got you up fast. We should try that in math class. Maybe it'll keep you awake for once."

Serena rubbed her throbbing head and frowned. Just her luck, she thought sadly. She had to be unconscious when a cute guy was around. If only she'd stayed asleep a little longer, maybe he would've come to take care of her. After all, she was a damsel in distress.

Raye patted Serena's arm. "Are you OK?" Raye asked. "I'm sorry, I felt an evil presence, and I mistakenly thought it was you."

Serena gazed at Raye, and couldn't help but stare at the priestess' cool dark eyes. They reminded

Serena of a lake at night, when the deep water was dark and shimmering.

"I'll live," Serena replied.

"Are you sure you're OK?" Molly asked.

"OK?" A sly grin crossed Serena's face. "How can I be OK when there's a gorgeous guy around here who I haven't seen yet. So, where is he?"

Serena looked over at Raye. "Point me in his direction. No hottie's getting away without me seeing him!"

Raye shrugged. "He does odd jobs around the temple. I suppose he's around here some-where."

"Is he your brother?" Molly asked.

Raye screwed her face. "He's a blond. Do you really think someone as dark-haired as I am could be his sister?"

Serena laughed. Raye had a little bit of an attitude, but she seemed really cool. And her priestess robes were fab. Serena hoped the Gap would come out with a priestess line one of these days. Forest green would look great on her.

"My grandfather's somewhat of a chatterbox," Raye said after a moment. "He always asking visitors if they want to work here. We don't need the help, he's just lonely." She shook her head. "The blond guy's name is J.J. He asked to work here, so, of course, my grandpa let him."

The priestess closed her eyes and sighed. "Anyway," she said softly, "I'm really sorry about attacking you, Serena. I sensed evil, but I was wrong. It wasn't you." She frowned. "I've been wrong a lot lately."

Serena's eyes widened. "So you can really sense evil?" she asked, amazed. "That is so cool! They should make a movie about you. It'd be like *The Sixth Sense*."

"No, it wouldn't," said Molly. "We saw *The Sixth Sense* together. It wasn't about sensing evil, it was about sensing dead people."

"Oh, forget *The Sixth Sense*. Our movie would be better, anyway. It would be about Raye, but we'd be in it, too. Don't you see? We'd be stars!"

Raye shook her head. Obviously, she hadn't hit Serena hard enough.

Raye rubbed her tired eyes. Serena, Molly,

mars attacks

and Lisa were still chatting excitedly about Raye's powers, but Raye wasn't listening. She brushed a strand of midnight hair from her face and stared blankly at the floor.

Luna sat in the far corner of the room, watching the priestess carefully. "I think," the cat murmured under her breath, "we may have just found someone very important."

Chapter 3
Demon Driver

Molly and Lisa left the Cherry Hill temple a little while later, but Serena stayed on to check the place out. After about an hour, she threw up her hands.

"Dang." She frowned. "Where is that blond babe?"

Luna growled. "I thought you were investigating, Serena!"

Serena laughed loudly and scratched her head. "I was investigating," she answered sweetly. "Didn't I say that? Yeah, sure, that's what I was doing." She giggled nervously. "Relax, Luna."

mars attacks

The cat growled and crossed her kitty arms. "I swear," she muttered. "Sometimes I think you're completely hopeless."

Serena rolled her eyes and stormed off in the direction of the bus stop. Hopeless, she thought. Luna seemed to be satisfied only with Amy, and there was no chance Serena was ever going to be as smart as Amy. Luna needed to realize that Amy was the brainy scout, and Serena was the fashion-conscious Sailor. It wasn't Serena's job to be smart.

"Serena!"

Serena turned and saw Amy dash across the street to join her. "Hey, Amy." Serena grinned.

"Hi," Amy answered, clutching her book bag as she ran up. She took a moment to catch her breath. "Find out anything?"

Serena flicked an angry look at Luna. "Only that this cat is bossier than Ms. Haruna. Luna wouldn't let me get a good luck charm."

"We don't have time for frivolous things," Luna snapped in her own defense. "Your purpose here is to investigate, not fool around."

Serena scowled. "Why can't I get a love charm while I'm here? You never let me enjoy anything."

"They may've sold out already." Amy pointed toward the bus stop. "Look."

Serena turned around to see a large group of teenage girls waiting for the 6 o'clock bus. Every single girl held a good luck charm in her hand.

"Wow!" Serena cried. "Those charms are so cute!" She just knew one of them would look fabulous on her backpack.

"Serena, grow up!" Luna ordered. "Amy, look at those girls. I think they're brainwashed!"

Serena shrugged off the insult, then squinted to get a better look. Sure enough, the schoolgirls looked like a bunch of zombies. They just stood there with the blankest of expressions on their faces.

Amy's eyes widened. "Those charms," she murmured. "They must be doing something to the girls." She checked her watch. This is the 666 line. The newspaper said that the 666 bus disappeared at 6 P.M. yesterday. It's 5:55 right now!"

Serena ground her teeth. The charms were a tool of the Enemy? Great. Now she'd never be able to get a charm. Those stupid bad guys ruined everything cool—though, if you were going to devise a scheme to suck up energy, Serena thought, you probably would start with hip, energetic teenagers like herself.

Luna stared at the zombified teens. "This is the bus that vanished yesterday," she said, "we have to get on and see where it goes."

"What?" Serena scowled. "But what if it disappears?"

"That's the whole point," Amy answered. The blue-haired girl turned to Serena. "We need to see where it's disappearing to."

Serena threw her hands up. "Fine!" she shouted as she stomped off toward the bus stop. She was tired of arguing. Besides, after missing the hottie J.J., and losing out on getting a love charm, disappearing couldn't make the day much worse.

The bus pulled up to the stop a few minutes later. Serena waited for the mob to board, but when her turn came, she hesitated.

"Um, I don't think we should do this," she whispered as she took a step back.

"What's wrong?" Amy asked as she gave Serena a nudge towards the door. "Don't be scared,

Serena. We're all going together."

"The bus driver," she said nervously, "she's really freaky-looking."

Serena pointed to the bus driver, a woman with a sharply angled face and a low-brimmed hat—she looked like a psycho from an old horror movie.

Luna growled. "Serena, get on!"

The bus driver turned to look at them. She pushed up her hat, gave a sadistic grin, and said, "All aboard."

"Yagh!" Serena jumped back. "No way," she declared, shaking her head violently. "Forget it. I'm not going." The last thing Serena wanted was to vanish and end up in netherspace with that woman.

Amy took Serena by the arm. "Serena," she whispered quickly. "Come on or we'll miss it!"

"I'm not going!" Serena said angrily, breaking from Amy's hold. "Go ahead and disappear with that Marilyn Manson lookalike if you want, but there's no way I'm getting on."

The driver closed the door, and the bus drove away.

mars attacks

"There goes our chance." Amy sighed.

"Serena." Luna scowled. "I can't believe you. That was our chance to find out what's going on."

"Oh my God!" Amy screamed. She pointed a finger at the retreating bus. "Look!"

Serena turned around, and froze. The bus was floating in mid-air.

"It's being abducted!" Luna shouted.

A black portal formed in front of the bus. The bus flew through it and disappeared into the blackness. The portal shrunk, and then it, too, disappeared into the void.

Amy's jaw dropped open. Serena's eyes went wide.

"No way," Serena whispered in disbelief. "The bus actually vanished into thin air!"

The next afternoon, Serena was back at the Cherry Hill temple. She dashed up the last few steps with Luna right behind her. Raye was feeding some black crows—the birds were taking the seeds right out of the priestess' hand.

"Raye!" Serena cried.

She ran to the priestess, panting heavily. "Raye, thank God you're here. The 666 bus vanished again!"

Raye looked up. Her eyes were cold. "Yeah, Serena," she said harshly. "Everyone's been here today because of that."

Serena gave a start. She could see that Raye was angry, she just didn't know why.

Maybe Raye had found out about the tapestry Serena had accidentally knocked off the wall while investigating the temple the day before. Man, Serena thought, the last thing she wanted was to have a priestess with supernatural powers mad at her.

"Raye," Serena said carefully. "I just wanted to ask a few questions. That was the second bus on that line to disappear, and since all the girls on that bus were holding good luck charms from this temple—"

"You think it's our fault, right?" Raye stood up and glared at the blonde. "Go ahead and say it. The police were here earlier, and so were the parents of those girls. Everybody's blaming the temple for those buses."

mars attacks

Serena's mouth dropped open. Raye was really angry.

"Uh, no," Serena stammered, "I don't think—"

"You all think I made those buses disappear with my powers." Raye clenched her fists. "Let me tell you something," she said darkly, "I was born with my sixth sense; I never asked for it. But I'd never use it for evil."

She turned her back to Serena, and continued to feed the crows. "Those stupid charms were J.J.'s idea, so leave me alone."

Serena felt bad for Raye. Everyone was blaming the priestess, but Serena knew that Raye would never do something evil like making people disappear.

"I'm sorry," the blonde said quietly. "I didn't mean to accuse you, Raye. I know you didn't do anything."

Serena turned and slowly walked back down the temple stairs. She called back to Luna, "Come on."

Luna paused a moment, taking a long look at the priestess. Raye angrily brushed a strand of hair from her face and tapped her sandaled feet. Suddenly, Luna jumped into the air, spun around, and dropped a little red pen in a flurry of scarlet and orange lights. She nudged the pen toward Raye, then ran after Serena.

Raye felt something bump into her foot. She looked down. The priestess picked up the pen and examined it. She twirled it around in her fingers. "What's this?"

The pen only sparkled in reply.

The 666 bus stop was crowded with the usual suspects—a group of half-asleep, charm-wielding, zombie-like teenage girls. Serena stood behind them, holding Luna close.

"All I know," Serena whispered, "is that Raye is not responsible for this."

Luna nodded. "I agree. It's not Raye, but maybe someone else at the temple is behind it all."

Serena bit her fingernail. She thought for a moment. It couldn't be Raye's grandfather, he seemed harmless enough. And then there was that blond hottie J.J.

Serena froze. "Oh no," she whispered, covering her mouth. "Don't tell me..."

"What?" Luna asked.

"How stupid can I be?" Serena groaned. "A mysterious blond babe shows up and bad stuff starts happening. It's like all the times before." She slapped her forehead. "J.J. is Jedite!"

The bus drove up. The door opened, and the girls began to board.

"We'll have to deal with Jedite later," Luna whispered as she jumped onto Serena's shoulder. "For now, we have to get on this bus and see where it's going."

Serena shook her head—she could feel herself start to panic. "But Amy said she'd come, and she's not here yet."

"We'll have to go without her, then." Luna pointed toward the bus. "Go."

Serena gulped and looked at the driver. It was the same evil-looking lady from before. Serena stepped back.

"No way, Luna," she said nervously. "I'm not going without Amy. That lady freaks me out."

Luna jumped to the ground and grabbed Serena's sock in her teeth.

"Serena, we're going to miss it again!" the cat cried, as she tried desperately to pull Serena onto the bus. "If you're so scared, then use the Luna Pen and transform. Suck it up, Serena, we have to get on!"

"Oh yeah!" Serena exclaimed. "The Luna Pen."

She reached into her dress pocket and pulled it out. She wouldn't be as scared if she could transform into someone who was less of a wimp than plain old Serena Tsukino.

"MOON POWER!" Serena shouted as she held her pen high. "TRANSFORM INTO A GORGEOUS FLIGHT ATTENDANT!"

The bus had already started down the street when Serena's clothes melted into a navy-blue uniform. Her ponytails were gone, and a cute navy-blue hat rested between her hair buns.

"A flight attendant?" Luna asked with a growl as the two ran after the bus. "Do you need glasses?"

"Luna," Serena yelled, "if we're gonna get on that bus, we're gonna have to fly."

With that, Serena and Luna leapt for the bus.

Chapter 4
Playing With Fire

Serena jumped from the bus as soon as it stopped its descent. Luna landed beside her.

"Where are we?" the Champion of Justice whispered as she gazed at their surroundings. "This place is creepy."

The black vortex had brought them to a cold, silent place. It was dark and barren like the surface of a distant planet. The three missing buses hovered lifelessly a few feet above the ground. The passengers remained unconscious, their energy completely drained from them.

Another portal suddenly appeared.

Serena's eyes widened as a girl dropped from it and fell through the air.

"Raye!" Serena shouted.

The psycho bus driver jumped from the bus and caught the priestess mid-air. The bus driver's clothes melted into old rags, and her skin turned green. She sneered as she wrapped an arm around Raye's neck.

"Ew!" Serena took a step back. "That lady is just so nasty!'

"Serena, transform!" Luna ordered as Raye fought against the monster-driver's grip. "You have to save Raye!"

Serena scowled. It was bad enough, she thought, that Jedite had set up Raye, getting her blamed for the missing buses. Now, they were kidnapping her, too? They'd gone too far.

"How dare you hurt Raye!" Serena cried as she thrust a finger at the nasty lady. "You bad guys have caused her enough trouble. Prepare to get fried! MOON PRISM POWER MAKE-UP!"

Lights flashed like a Friday night dance club, and rainbow colors wrapped around Serena as her flight attendant's uniform morphed into a sailor suit. When the lights died down, Raye could not believe her eyes.

"Sailor Moon?!"

Serena struck her traditional super-hero pose. She was looking forward to zapping that freaky-bus-driver-lady-monster-type-creature.

"You've given a bad name to all the hard-working bus drivers in our city," Serena declared. "I am Sailor Moon, Champion of Justice and defender of public transportation, and on behalf of the moon, you're punished!"

"Little brat!" The monster snarled as she gripped Raye tighter. "Surrender, or I'll choke her."

Serena bared her teeth. "That's low!" she shouted as she pulled off her tiara. "Let Raye go, you Resident Evil reject!"

Raye fought against the monster's hold.

"Stay back!" Raye cried, as her forehead began to glow. "Sailor Moon, don't put yourself in danger because of me! I'll fight her off myself!"

A red symbol, a heart with an arrow shooting from it, appeared on Raye's forehead. Serena's jaw dropped.

"Luna!" The Champion of Justice spun

around to face her cat. "Is that—"

Luna ran to Raye, shouting: "Raye! Use your pen! You are Sailor Mars!"

The cat then turned to the dumbfounded Serena. "Quickly, use your tiara to trap the monster!"

Serena turned toward the struggling priestess. "Raye's a Sailor Scout?"

All right, Serena thought. Now there would be even less work for Sailor Moon—she had two partners!

Serena threw her tiara with all her might. "MOON TIARA ACTION...TRAP!"

The glowing tiara streaked through the air. It shot down over the monster, pinning her arms to her sides. The evil bus driver roared as Raye managed to drop to the ground and roll away.

"Stupid girl!" the villain cried as she fought to get free.

Serena ran to Raye and helped her up. "You OK?" the Champion of Justice asked.

Raye eyed Sailor Moon closely. "Is that you Serena?" she whispered.

"Yeah, it's me. How do you like being a

mars attacks

Sailor Scout?"

Raye looked over at the monster. "That creature's breaking free," the priestess said quickly as
the villain slid the tiara down her body. "What do
we do?"

"The pen!" Luna ordered, taking a kitty's
fighting stance. "Raye, use the pen I gave you.
Hold it to the sky and shout 'MARS POWER
MAKE-UP!'"

Raye gave a start. "The cat talks?"

"Raye," Serena ordered, "do what she says.
She knows more about this super-hero stuff than I
do."

Serena turned to the monster, only to see the
creature push the tiara to her feet and kick it off.

"Raye!" Serena cried. "Hurry!"

Raye reached into her sleeve and pulled out
her pen. She thrust it into the air.

"MARS POWER...MAKE-UP!"

Fiery red light burst from the pen and
washed over Raye's body. She closed her eyes as
fire rings encircled her, melting her priestess robes
into a red and white Sailor Scout uniform, complete with matching scarlet earrings and high-

heeled boots.

"Wow, Raye, what a great look," Serena said. "That outfit just screams 'super-hero.'"

The monster snarled and clenched her fist. "Sailor Scout or no Sailor Scout, you girls are history!"

Luna, as always, was fully prepared with a flawless battle plan. "Mars," she commanded, "use your weapon! Your powers are fire-based. Aim at the monster and shout 'MARS FIRE IGNITE!'"

The monster prepared to attack, but Raye was faster. The priestess' dark eyes flashed purple as she clasped her hands together. She shot her index fingers out and aimed for the villain, flames gathered around her fingertips.

"MARS FIRE…IGNITE!"

Flames ripped through the air and engulfed the monster. The villain screamed as the fire burned her to ashes.

Serena looked at the smoldering pile of dust on the ground. "That was quick. She didn't even have time to threaten us or curse us for all eternity."

Raye brushed the dust off her hands. "I don't like to waste time," she answered flatly.

mars attacks

Serena smiled. Raye was unlike anyone else Serena had ever met. It wasn't just toughness, Serena thought, it was power. Her eyes, Serena thought as she stared at Raye, her eyes show so much power. Raye was going to make a fabulous addition to the Sailor Scout team.

Serena suddenly felt something stir deep inside her, something that made her uneasy. True, Serena felt safer now that Raye was a Sailor Scout, knowing Raye would look out for her. But when Serena thought about having a protector, it was almost as if a dark hole had opened up in her heart. Whatever it was, Serena didn't want to think about it.

"Hello?"

Serena gave a start, realizing Raye was staring at her. Serena shook her head to clear it.

"Sorry," she mumbled, offering no further explanation.

Raye shook her head. "Daydreaming?" she asked. "At a time like this? We have to get these buses back to Crossroads, Sailor Moon."

Serena gave a half-hearted smile and threw up her hands. "Exactly what I was thinking," she answered.

Luna rolled her eyes. "Sure you were."

Chapter 5
Nightmare Land

Queen Beryl's long, slender fingers clenched the stone armrests of her throne. Jedite kneeled before her.

"You are a disgrace," she said with a snarl. "I should dispose of you now."

Jedite closed his eyes and lowered his head. "Forgive me, my queen."

"Keep your mouth shut!" Beryl's eyes burned with anger. "You tell me you're going to destroy the Sailor Scouts, and instead a third one shows up?! You're a failure and a traitor to our

40

cause!"

Jedite was silent, though his gloved hand clenched into a fist.

"You're running low on chances," Beryl warned. "Continue to fail me, and you will be sorry."

Beryl pressed her hands against a crystal ball. A ray of light burst forth from the crystal—a hologram projected the image of the three Sailor Scouts.

"Sailor Moon, Mercury, Mars." Beryl thrust a long-nailed finger at the image. "I don't know what they're after, but I want them gone."

"Of course," Jedite answered softly. If the general was nervous, he didn't show it. "I have another plan that will gather energy, as well as destroy those Sailor Scouts. It has been set into motion, I've already gathered the energy of fifty humans."

Beryl sat back in her throne and waved a hand. "Proceed with your plan," she ordered. "But do not fail me again. You are not indispensable, Jedite."

Jedite nodded. "Understood."

Serena relaxed and crossed her arms behind her head. She pointed her sock-covered toes, and leaned back against Raye's bed.

"Raye, your room is perfect for lounging," she said with a grin. "I didn't know temples could have such great vegging rooms."

Or that a priestess could be so with the times, she added to herself. Raye's walls were plastered with posters of Nine Inch Nails, Buffy, and The X-Files. Fantasy novels were stacked on her desk. It looked like living in a temple didn't keep Raye from acting like a normal, hip teenager.

And better yet, Amy and Raye had hit if off immediately. They seemed to understand each other well. Serena was glad to see that they both took their Sailor Scout roles so seriously—somebody had to.

Raye sat on top of the bed. Instead of her usual priestess robes, she wore a stylish CK blouse and a pair of Levi's. "I need a place to relax," she said as she casually brushed a strand of hair from her face. "My workload gets heavy sometimes, so I fixed this room up to be nice and stress-free."

mars attacks

"A wise decision," Amy remarked as she flipped through a newspaper. "Relaxation is essential to a healthy lifestyle."

"You can say that again." Serena grinned. "In fact, I think relaxing is more important than anything."

Luna hopped into Serena's lap and scowled. "Coulda seen that one coming," the cat muttered. "Serena's philosophy is 'All play and no work makes a happy Sailor Scout.'"

Serena laughed. "You're finally beginning to understand me, Luna." She picked up a comic book resting by her side and glanced at the cover.

"You have a subscription to Sailor V?!" Serena shrieked as she jumped up, sending Luna sprawling onto the floor. She flipped through the comic in a whirlwind of pages. "Cool!"

Serena was impressed. This issue had come out just the day before. Serena was thrilled to find out she wasn't the only Sailor Scout into Sailor V.

Raye sat up quickly. "Hey," she snapped. "I haven't read that one yet." She yanked the comic out of Serena hands. "I don't let anyone read my comics until I've gone through them at least once."

Serena was about to reply, but Raye knocked her over with a pillow. "Luna?" the priestess asked, "what is it we're supposed to do as Scouts? You said there was a Moon Princess."

Serena angrily threw the pillow off and slumped back to the floor. She couldn't believe it. How rude, she thought, Raye could really be annoying.

"There is a Moon Princess," Luna answered, "but I don't know much about her except that we need to find her. You three will need to work together to find her and protect her from the forces of evil."

Serena groaned. "All we need," she muttered flatly, "a damsel in distress to take care of."

Raye shot a glance at Serena. "Based on what Amy tells me, we'll have our hands full taking care of you."

Serena eyes sparkled dangerously. "Watch it, chick."

Amy opened her newspaper and turned it around for all to see. "While Luna's gathering information on the Princess," she remarked, "we should be doing our job."

mars attacks

"What job?" Serena asked.

"Our job helping the innocent," Amy said, exasperated. "Look at this."

Serena leaned forward. Amy pointed to an article—DREAMLAND SUFFERS NIGHTMARE. A picture of an amusement park accompanied the article.

Amusement park? Serena thought, brightening. That actually sounds like a fun assignment. A nice change from disappearing buses and their psycho drivers.

"This new theme park just opened," Amy explained. "In this past week, fifty people have disappeared without a trace."

Raye crossed her arms. "Sounds like the Enemy."

"Exactly." Amy nodded.

Serena hopped to her feet. "Great idea!" she declared as she grabbed her purse from the bed. "I'm having a wicked craving for cotton candy, so let's get going."

Luna's eyes flickered dangerously. "Serena," the cat said, clenching a kitty paw, "this isn't a field trip. You're going to investigate, don't forget that."

Serena rolled her eyes. Luna was definitely the biggest party crasher on the planet. If that bossy cat was going to keep Serena from having any fun, she was going to end up with one crabby Sailor Moon. And how could a crabby Champion of Justice defend the innocent?

"You gotta loosen up, Luna." Serena slid open Raye's door and stepped through it. "You keep worrying like this, and you're gonna end up with lots of gray hairs in that black coat of yours."

Luna opened her mouth to reply, but Amy quickly covered the cat's mouth with her hand.

"Anyway," Amy said, "we should get going. Ready, Raye?"

Raye shook her head. "Great," she muttered. "One food-crazy boy-chaser, and one seriously-bossy guardian cat. I can see being a Sailor Scout is going to be loads of fun."

Amy shrugged as she stroked Luna's fur. "You get used to it."

A mob of reporters crowded around the Dreamland entrance. A blond man in a guard's uniform kept his hat brim low over his eyes as he stood before the microphones.

"Is it true fifty people disappeared from Dreamland this week?" one reporter asked.

The guard shook his head. "No," he answered. "No one has disappeared from here. We keep track of how many people come in and out every day, and everyone's accounted for."

"But people are claiming their loved ones came to this park and never came home!" another reporter shouted. "How can you say--"

"If anyone's disappeared, they disappeared on their way home from the park, not inside the park." The guard waved a hand. "We have nothing to do with people disappearing. Please go home."

The reporters mumbled angrily and shoved their recorders back into their belts. As the crowd turned and slowly shuffled from the park entrance, the guard tipped up his hat.

Jedite bared his teeth as he smiled. "Fools," he whispered under his breath.

Chapter 6
No Lion Down
on the Job

Serena's ponytails bobbed behind her as she ran to the entrance of Dreamland. She dumped her purse on the ticket-seller's counter and grinned. "One ticket, please."

The woman behind the counter nodded and took Serena's money. Serena could barely contain her excitement. She hadn't been to a theme park in a long time.

This was going to be great, she thought. They had a roller coaster. And a Ferris wheel. And that game with the mallets where you whack the mole. Serena grabbed the ticket and ran through the entrance. The guard at the gate kept his hat low over his eyes as Serena passed.

Dreamland was a new theme park. There were dozens of rides, tons of games, and, best of all, lots of food stands.

Serena punched a fist into her palm and smiled. "All right!" she exclaimed. "Party time!"

"Excuse me, what did you just say?"

Serena turned around slowly to see an angry Luna glaring up at her. Amy and Raye stood just behind Luna.

Just my luck, Serena thought. A perfect day of fun ruined by the doomsday patrol.

"I said," Serena muttered sarcastically, "'all right, investigation time.'"

"Good," Raye snapped as she crossed her arms. "People have been disappearing, Serena. This isn't the place to have fun."

"Raye," Serena said through clenched teeth, "you are really starting to sound like Luna. You guys need to get some sugar into you, because now you're starting to depress me."

Luna jumped out of Amy's arms and looked up at the girls. "All right," the cat ordered, "listen

4 9

up. We need a plan of action. Amy, you read the article about this place?"

Amy nodded.

"Good. Was there anything that may tell us where the people were last seen before disappearing?"

"No," Amy replied. "The police are baffled by it. It's almost as if they vanished into thin air."

"Oh, no," said Serena, "not that again."

"I could walk around and see if I can sense any evil vibes," Raye offered. The priestess hooked her thumbs into her jeans' pockets. "Since I became Sailor Mars, my sixth sense has been really reliable. I should be able to feel any evil that's around here."

Luna nodded. "Good. We'll split up. Amy comes with me, and Raye will go with—"

Luna stopped in mid-sentence. The Champion of Justice was gone. Luna turned red with anger. " Serena!"

Amy spotted Serena first, at a snack stand. The Champion of Justice was scarfing down a huge pink cloud of cotton candy while hugging two large pretzels, a super huge popcorn, a Sprite, and three hot dogs with The Works.

mars attacks

The blue-haired girl shook her head. "Looks like Serena's trying a new approach to carbo-loading."

Raye shook her head. "I got her," she muttered as she walked toward the snack stand. She glanced back over her shoulder at Amy and Luna. "You two get going. We'll meet up at two o'clock."

"Remember," Amy called, "have patience."

Raye had tried to take away Serena's snacks, but Serena had complained so loudly that the priestess had eventually given up and let the blonde pig out. As they walked through the park, Raye kept her eyes peeled for any signs of evil while Serena downed her food in record speed.

The Champion of Justice popped the last piece of pretzel into her mouth. "Y'know," she mumbled as she chewed, "these pretzels are really good. I'm gonna get another. Want one, Raye?"

Raye glared at her. "Serena," she said flatly, "you're disgusting. How could you think of food after chowing down like that?" She motioned at the theme park around them. "We're supposed to be checking this place for any signs of danger.

Focus!"

Serena scowled. "I am focused."

"Focused on making a pig out of yourself, you mean." Raye let out a breath, exasperated. "I can see why Luna gets so tired of you. You have no idea how to deal with respons--" Raye stopped in mid-sentence, Serena was gone again.

Raye stomped her foot. "Argh! Where is she?"

Serena laughed from behind Raye. "Cool!" the blonde exclaimed. "I haven't been on one of these in years!"

Raye whipped around to see Serena riding on a carousel. The priestess ran over to the ride and pulled Serena off her horse.

"Serena," Raye said with a hiss, "you aren't even listening to me! What's wrong with you?"

Serena broke from Raye's grip and stepped back angrily. "Nothing's wrong with me," she said. "I just wanna have a little fun, and you're being majorly cranky. Let loose and relive your childhood a little."

"I don't think you ever grew out of your childhood." Raye scowled. "Come on," she ordered as she walked away. "We only have a few hours to cover this park."

This was totally unfair, Serena thought. Raye was like a drill sergeant. Serena's wasn't going to get to go on any rides. The whole point of a theme park was to have fun. Not partying at a theme park was like a Wendy's Cheeseburger Deluxe without the cheese. It went against nature.

Serena was so deep in thought, she didn't realize something nuzzling against her foot. "Huh?" she murmured, looking down. A huge lion was playing with her shoelace.

"AAAAAIIIIIIIIIIII!!!" Serena jumped onto Raye's shoulders and wrapped her legs around the priestess' neck. "A lion!" she screamed. "Oh my God, it's gonna eat me! Kill it, Raye!"

Raye choked as she tried to unwrap Serena's legs from her throat. "Serena!" she coughed "Can't...breathe!"

A pretty young woman, in a frilly pink dress and sparkling crown, walked up to Serena. "It's all right," she said, laughing. "Please, don't be frightened. It's not a real lion, it's just a robot."

Serena stopped screaming and looked over

at the woman, who held a large red apple.

"A robot?" Serena asked.

The young woman nodded. "Yes. We have lots of robotic animals around here for the people to play with." She smiled and introduced herself. "I'm the Dream Princess, the mascot of this park."

Serena let go of Raye. Robots? Cool, Serena thought. It was like Gundam, only in real life. Well, fluffy animal robots weren't really like giant fighting Gundam units, but they were still robots, and robots were majorly cool.

"I've never seen walking robots like that," Serena exclaimed.

The princess smiled and pointed to the lion. "You can play with him," she explained. "He even talks, all the animals do." The pink-haired woman waved her hand over the apple she held—the fruit glowed white.

Serena's eyes widened as robotic rabbits, squirrels, and deer walked up. She bent down and scratched a deer under the chin. "You're so cute!" she cried. "Oh, Raye, come see! They're adorable."

"Hello," the deer said in a cutesy robot voice. Serena laughed.

"These are so cool!" She turned around. "Raye, why don't you come over?"

But Raye was staring at the Dream Princess suspiciously. A little boy walked up to a robotic bear and started petting it.

"Stay away from that," Raye said quickly as she took the boy's arm and pulled him away. "It's not safe."

Great, Serena thought, now she's even ruining the fun of a little kid she's never met. Raye was way out of line.

"Excuse me," Serena said shortly as she yanked the boy from Raye's hand. "Of course it's safe. The Dream Princess said it was."

Raye narrowed her eyes. "Well, I don't trust the Dream Princess," she murmured as she grabbed the boy back. She lowered her voice. "I'm getting evil vibes from her, Serena."

"What?" Serena rolled her eyes. "Right. And I suppose you think that petite little princess is behind the disappearances?"

"Maybe."

Serena scoffed. "Get real, Raye." No way could such a sweet and pretty lady make people vanish.

"You're just paranoid," Serena said with a snarl as she pulled the boy to her. "This kid's gonna ride the bear and have fun."

"No." Raye grabbed him back. "It's not safe."

Serena's eyes flashed with anger. "Yes." She yanked the boy. "He is."

"No he's not."

"Yes he is!"

"No he's not!"

"Yes he is!"

"No he's no--"

"What do you think you're doing to my son?"

Serena and Raye froze. A woman stood above them, eyes burning.

"Um…" Raye gently pushed the boy back to his mother. "Sorry."

The woman took her son by the hand and stomped away.

Serena blushed and scratched her head. "Oops," she muttered.

Chapter 7
When Sweet
Dreams Turn Sour

Serena made herself comfortable in her little pink plastic seat. She and Raye were riding the Kiddy Train, a string of pink and orange cars that choo-chooed through Dreamland on a little track. A group of little kids ahead of them squealed with glee.

Serena didn't care if she looked dorky, at least she didn't have to walk. Her feet were killing her. Raye had dragged her around the park for a whole hour looking for evil. If she couldn't be screaming with delight on one of Dreamland's twelve roller coasters, at least she was getting a chance to relax.

"What a waste," Raye called from the seat behind Serena. "I think we should get back to walking. We'll cover more ground."

"Will you give it up, Raye?" Serena said with a growl. "Cut me some slack. I'm exhausted and bored. The least you could do is let me get off my feet for a few minutes."

Raye narrowed her eyes. "Don't think I enjoy spending my free time wandering around a theme park looking for the Enemy. I have enough work at the temple as it is, and this is supposed to be my day off." Raye rested back in her seat. "This is duty, Serena."

Serena clenched her teeth. Duty was so boring. Why couldn't it be their duty to play the games and ride the attractions? That would be a duty she could really enjoy.

The Kiddy Train suddenly jerked to a halt. Serena fell forward, crashing into the tall man sitting in front of her.

"Sorry," the robotic panda bear driver called from the head of the train. "We're experiencing a slight technical difficulty, folks. Sit tight and we'll have it fixed in a few minutes."

mars attacks

Serena rubbed her aching nose and sat back in her seat. "That hurt," the blonde whined. "Geez, this thing is dangerous."

The man turned around. "I think it's just your lack of balance that's dangerous."

Serena's eyes widened. Oh God, she thought. Not him again!

But it was him—the dark-haired creep who always seemed to pop up when Serena was at her most embarrassed. Making fun of her seemed to be the guy's favorite pastime. She usually bumped into him around Crossroads. What was he doing here?

Serena threw up her hands. "I don't believe it!" she exclaimed. "I come onto a train made for five-year-olds, and I still manage to bump into you!"

The dark-haired guy was as fashionable as ever, clad in a black, short-sleeved Ralph Lauren polo shirt and Dockers khakis. He smiled sarcastically. "If this train's for five-year-olds," he asked, "why are you on it?"

Serena's eyes blazed. "None of your business!" she shouted. "And what about you?"

The guy was at least a few years older than Serena. What kind of a teenage loser made fun of middle-school girls and rode Kiddy Trains?

He grinned. "I'm young at heart," he cooed. "And stop shouting, Meatball Head. You're foaming at the mouth."

Raye, who was watching the whole episode from the back of the train, raised an eyebrow with interest.

Serena felt the steam blowing out of her ears. Her hair buns did not look like meatballs—they were stylish. In fact, they were so stylish, she was the only one chic enough to wear them. Her hairstyle was a Serena original.

"You obviously don't know good hair when you see it!" Serena cried as the train started up again.

"I'm getting off here," he called as he jumped off the train. He winked at Serena as the train chugged past. "Don't eat yourself sick, blondie. I can just picture you scarfing hot dogs and then going on the Tsunami Coaster and puking your guts out."

Serena shook a fist as they rode away. "Stay

away from me!" she yelled as he disappeared into the park. "I don't want to waste my time arguing with a loser like you!"

His laughter trailed behind him.

Serena crossed her arms and scowled. "He's such a jerk," she muttered. She took a deep breath to calm her thumping heart.

"Your boyfriend?"

Serena spun around to look at Raye. "What?!" she screamed.

"Well, he was good-looking." Raye shrugged.

"You're kidding me!" Serena cried. "Raye, you've either been in the sun too long, or your taste in guys is just totally whack. There was absolutely nothing attractive about that creep!"

As if, Serena thought angrily as she turned back around and pressed her lips tight. That jerk cute? No way! And even though he did have thick midnight hair and ocean blue eyes, that didn't mean...

Serena swallowed as her heart sped up. OK, she thought quickly. So he's got pretty eyes, so what? He was still a sleazeball, and she still hated him. Boyfriend? Hmph. She didn't even care to know his name.

The panda train driver looked over his shoulder. "Next stop is the Sweet Dream Factory," he called. "The one o'clock party will be starting soon. The Dream Princess will be welcoming all her guests with cookies and candies."

"The Dream Princess?" Raye repeated quietly. "She was the only one I felt an evil force from. We should check it out."

Serena could already feel the drool coming. Free cookies, free candy--that would definitely be a good place to investigate!

"Yeah!" Serena agreed. " Let's go to that Sweet Dream Factory and pig ou--I mean, check it out!"

Raye scowled. "An hour ago, you insisted the Dream Princess was harmless. Why'd you suddenly change your mind?"

Serena didn't answer, but Raye understood when she saw the wicked smile that curled Serena's lips.

"Food," Raye said darkly. "It seems the only way to get you to do anything is to lure you in with food." Raye shook her head. "Which means," she muttered to herself, "if the Enemy ever decides to set a trap with donuts as bait, we're history."

Amy glanced around the main room of the Sweet Dreams Factory. It looked like a castle, with high ceilings and white marble pillars that shone under the bright lights. Tables covered with cookies, candies, and cakes filled the room. Children scurried around grabbing as many treats as their hands and stomachs could hold.

"There are a lot of people here," Amy noted as more visitors poured through the doors. "Has to be close to fifty."

The number sounded familiar to Amy. "Fifty!" She gasped. "That's how many people disappeared earlier this week." Her navy eyes scanned the room. "Could this be the place where they disappear from?"

The double doors to the Factory slowly swung shut. Amy clenched her teeth as all the children began to cheer.

The Dream Princess appeared on a small stage at the front of the room. "Hello!" she called cheerfully. "Parents and children alike, welcome to the party!"

The audience clapped. Amy reached into her pocket and touched her transformation pen.

The Dream Princess stepped off the stage and smiled. "So nice to see so many people here," said the princess. "Let me make you more comfortable."

The princess blew a red gas from her mouth, and it filled up the room quickly. Amy coughed and tried to shield her eyes with her arm.

When the gas disappeared, Amy looked up. She couldn't believe her eyes. They were no longer inside. The Sweet Dreams Factory had turned into a large field of wildflowers and butterflies. The visitors laughed and began playing in the open grass.

Amy's eyes widened. "Impossible," she said under her breath. "It must be an illusion."

"That'd be the drugged sweets," the Dream Princess said quietly.

Amy whipped around to see the princess standing behind her. "You're no mascot!" Amy yelled. The blue-haired girl narrowed her eyes.

6 4

mars attacks

"Who are you?"

"Like I'd tell you. Someone's looking for trouble." The princess waved a hand over her apple. "And you found it, chick."

The apple glowed white, and the Dream Princess smiled. "Your energy is mine," she said as the apple began to suck in a pearly light from everyone in the room.

Amy gasped. She tried to pull out her transformation pen, but her eyes suddenly went blurry. She fell to her knees. "No!" she cried.

"It doesn't matter what you know, little girl." The Dream Princess snickered. "Like the rest of these saps, you will never leave here. Sweet dreams."

Amy tried to stand, but it was no use.

"No!" Amy choked as she faltered. "Serena... Raye... the princess is... the one..."

Amy couldn't stay awake any longer. She fell to the floor, and everything went black.

The last thing she heard was the Dream Princess laughing.

Chapter 8
An Apple A Day Keeps
The Doctor Away

Raye looked up at the silent pink and orange castle that was the Sweet Dreams Factory. "There's evil here," she murmured. "I can feel it."

Serena didn't care if there was evil there, all she knew was that its huge doors were already locked. Serena pounded on them angrily.

No fair, she thought. The cookies and candies were in there. Why was there never a wrecking ball around when you needed one?

"Serena! Raye!" Luna appeared from the back of the Factory, and ran toward her Champions. "Girls, thank goodness you're here!"

mars attacks

"Luna, what is it?" Raye asked.

"Amy went inside to check out the party." Luna panted, nearly out of breath. "But the doors locked behind her and there's no other way in. There was a crowd of people inside, but now the whole place is silent!"

Raye stood up slowly. "That's it then," she said as she pulled out her transformation pen. "The Dream Princess is behind it, and this is where she's making the people vanish."

Serena's eyes widened. No way, she thought. The Dream Princess really was the villain?

"Transform," Luna ordered, stepping back from the girls. "You both need to hurry and get inside."

"Right." Raye looked around to make sure no one was watching, then thrust her pen into the sky.

"MARS POWER MAKE-UP!"

Fire swarmed over Raye and engulfed her in rings of scarlet and orange. She twirled as her Sailor Mars suit formed on her body.

Serena opened her hand. "MOON PRISM

POWER MAKE-UP!"

Rainbow lights swirled around her. Her Old Navy tee shirt and zipper flares melted into Sailor Moon's shining uniform.

Raye wasted no time. As soon as Serena's transformation had ended, the priestess clasped her hands together.

"MARS FIRE..." She pointed at the locked door. "IGNITE!"

Fire bolted from her fingertips and smashed through the door. Serena, Raye, and Luna ran through the blasted doorway and into the Sweet Dreams Factory. Before them, halls led in several directions.

"Which way?" Serena asked.

Raye shook her head. "It doesn't matter." She clenched her teeth. "I can feel the evil coming towards us, be on your guard."

"You can stop right there," called a voice.

Raye, Luna and Serena all screeched to a halt. Serena whipped her head around, her eyes scanning the dark hallway. "Who said that?" she shouted.

Red gas began to swirl through the air.

mars attacks

"Doesn't matter," the voice cooed. "Nothing matters. Don't be afraid, everything will be all right."

Serena coughed, and her vision grew hazy. As the gas seeped into her nose and mouth, she slowly relaxed.

Smells like candy, she thought sleepily. Very nice, she grinned to herself as her eyelids grew heavy.

"Sailor Moon!" Raye called from nearby. "Don't be fooled! It's an illusion!"

Serena didn't hear Raye as the dark hallway turned into a field of beautiful flowers. The Dream Princess was waiting there for Serena, as beautiful and kind as could be.

"Dear Sailor Moon," the Dream Princess cooed. She walked up to Serena holding a lovely wreath of daisies. "Welcome to happiness! There's no fighting here."

Serena smiled. "Really?" she murmured as the Dream Princess reached out to place the flower ring around Serena's neck.

Suddenly, Raye grabbed for the wreath, pushing the princess away from Serena. "Wake up!" Raye shouted. "It's--"

Raye was abruptly cut off as the flowers morphed into a long, slithering snake. Raye screamed as it bit into her arm.

Serena gasped. "Mars!" she cried. Serena grabbed the snake and threw it to the ground. The Dream Princess scowled as the serpent turned to stone.

As Raye clutched her injured arm, Serena bit her lip. She thought about how big an idiot she had been. Some Champion of Justice she was, Raye was hurt because Serena had ignored her responsibilities.

Raye's arm began to stiffen. Her gloved fingertips turned stony gray.

Luna ran up to Raye. "The snake!" Luna cried. "It was enchanted. Sailor Mars, break the spell with your priestess powers!"

Raye gritted her teeth and pulled a bit of parchment from her collar. It had an anti-evil charm written on it in symbols.

"That's like the thing you used at the temple," Serena said breathlessly.

The grayness had by now spread to Raye's

wrist. The priestess grunted against the pain. "My powers as a priestess include vanquishing evil spirits. Becoming Sailor Mars made my priestess powers stronger, so I may be able to break this spell."

The Dream Princess scoffed and crossed her arms. "Go ahead and try," she challenged. "It's no use. You'll be stone before you know it."

Serena glared at the evil woman. "Leave her alone!" the blonde snapped. "Mars is stronger than a Candy Land loser like you. And those pink frills on your dress are wicked tacky!"

Raye brought the parchment to her forehead. "Evil," she whispered lowly, "be gone! In the name of my temple and in the name of Mars, I banish you!"

The parchment glowed with power, and Raye slapped it onto her arm. Raye's dark eyes blazed purple.

"MARS FIRE IGNITE!

Light burst forth from the stone. In a flash of white, the stone cracked and fell from Raye's glove. She collapsed to the floor, panting.

"You did it!" Serena cried. She dropped to

her knees beside Raye. "You OK?"

Raye swallowed hard, then nodded. Serena wrapped her arms around Raye and squeezed gently.

"Thank God," Serena whispered. "I got worried for a second there."

Seeing Raye in such danger had suddenly made Serena want to take back all the mean things she had said to the priestess. Serena didn't realize how much she counted on Raye being with her.

Raye shrugged. "Nice to know you care," she answered quietly.

The Dream Princess narrowed her eyes. "Fine," she said. "Then it's time for the really big guns."

The woman closed her eyes. Her head shot down into her chest and disappeared. The princess' body began to spin. Her pink frilly dress dissolved into an evil-looking red and black metallic uniform.

"Be careful," Luna warned as Serena and Raye slowly got up. "We don't know what she's planning."

The Dream Princess' head popped back out

of her body, and spun around like a top. When it stopped, Serena saw that the princess' once-blue eyes were now metallic green, and her jaw was on hinges.

"So she's a robot, too." Serena punched her fist into her palm, determined. "Well, just as long as she isn't a Gundam, no problem."

The princess' green eyes glowed. "I am the Dream Dolly," she called in a metallic robot voice as she shot out another wave of red gas. "Prepare to be destroyed."

Serena and Raye threw their arms over their heads. "No!" Serena cried. "Not again!"

Raye gritted her teeth and clasped her hands together. "I'll get her," she said, aiming her index fingers at the robot. Raye narrowed her eyes. "MARS FIRE..."

The Dream Dolly blew another huge wave, and Raye cried out as red gas cut off her attack. Sailor Mars fell to the floor, coughing heavily.

Luna ran over to Raye and began licking her face.

Serena was coughing so hard she couldn't use her tiara. She grabbed her chest and squeezed shut her eyes. Everything was getting fuzzy, and the aroma of flowers wafted through the room.

"Another illusion." Serena coughed weakly. She opened her eyes a crack, and saw that the Sweet Dream Factory had again transformed into a field of flowers. "Luna, help!"

"Sailor Moon, don't give up," Luna called. "Mars has fallen into a spell, she needs you."

Serena gasped and looked at Raye. The priestess' eyes had rolled up into her head.

"NO!" Serena screamed.

Serena tried to get up, but she had no energy left. Her vision was getting blurry, and she could barely see the Dream Dolly raise her energy-zapping apple.

Suddenly, a flash of bright red streaked through the air—it was a red rose. The Dream Dolly dropped the apple as the sharp-tipped red rose pierced the Dolly's metallic shell. The robot began spinning out of control.

The gas began to disappear. Serena rubbed her eyes as the illusion faded. Her heart skipped when she saw the rose.

"Tuxedo Mask?" Serena whispered. But he

was nowhere to be seen.

When the gas cleared, Serena could see dozens of people lying unconscious on the floor—she recognized on of them. "Amy?"

"Amy!" Luna shouted as she ran over to the unconscious girl. "Amy, wake up!"

Luna turned to Serena. "She'll be OK. Go help on Raye."

Serena helped Raye to her feet. Serena hated to see her friends hurt, especially when she felt partially responsible. She turned to the princess and growled. "You are one annoying robot!"

Serena shot a finger out at the villain. It was time for one of her patented super-hero speeches. That stupid Dolly had toyed with them enough.

"You shattered the peace of a cheerful theme park, you demonic piece of metal. You're not gonna get away with that." Serena stood and flipped a ponytail over her shoulder in determination. "I am Sailor Moon, Champion of Justice and defender of the innocent, and on behalf of the moon, you're punished!"

The princess ran for the exit. Serena smiled

to herself. The robot had used an apple to drain their energy. Serena thought it was funny that Dolly's greatest weapon was a piece of fruit.

Amy groaned as Luna licked her face. The girl blinked her navy blue eyes and looked up.

"Amy," Raye called, keeping her dark eyes focused on the robot. "Are you all right?"

Amy nodded, standing up carefully. "Fine," she said shakily, glancing at the retreating princess. She narrowed her eyes. "But that girl's gotta go."

Serena smiled wickedly. "Then transform," she called. "Join the party, Ames!"

Amy nodded and pulled out her Mercury Pen. "Right," she said, thrusting the pen into the air.

"MERCURY POWER MAKE-UP!"

In ribbons of blue light, Amy's clothes liquefied into Sailor Mercury's suit. As soon as she had transformed, Amy cupped her hands together and formed a sphere of spinning blue light.

"MERCURY BUBBLES..." Amy pulled back and released the ball full force. "BLAST!"

The sphere burst into thick bubbles that surrounded the Dream Princess. Once the robot was distracted, Raye saw her chance.

"MARS FIRE..." Raye ran forward, whipping another parchment out. She jumped and slapped the parchment on the princess' forehead. "CHARGE!"

The princess made a metallic gasp. "What have you done? I can't move!"

Serena pulled off her headband. "Sayonara," she said darkly as she flung her weapon.

"MOON TIARA ACTION!"

Raye thrust out her index fingers. "MARS FIRE IGNITE!"

Raye's fire shot forward and wrapped around Serena's flying tiara. The burning disc crashed into the Dream Dolly, knocking her back. The robot's head popped off as a golden light traveled up her body.

"No!" It was the last thing the robot said before she exploding into a million pieces.

Serena crossed her arms. "Now that," she declared, "was cool. I didn't know your fire could merge with my tiara, Raye."

Luna nodded her approval. "Teamwork is

very important," the cat explained. "You're strong apart, but you're strongest together. To defeat the Enemy and find the Moon Princess, the Sailor Scouts must fight as a team."

Serena stretched out her arms. Things were going to work out after all, she thought as the unconscious victims began to awaken. Raye was bossy, but she and Serena had fought well together. Now, if Serena could only get her hands on one of Raye's comic books...

"Looks like everyone's coming around," Amy commented. She looked at Raye. "We should get going."

"Yeah." Raye rubbed her tired eyes. "We'd better go home. I'm exhausted."

Serena grinned widely and clapped her hands. "Tired?" she repeated. "You guys have gotta be kidding. Now that we beat the bad guy, we can go on the rides and pig out on junk food and hang at the games!" She ran out the door, calling behind her, "I'm getting more of those awesome pretzels. Anyone want one?"

"Geez." Raye frowned as she watched Serena disappear down the hallway. "Doesn't that girl ever give up?"

Amy smiled. "Not if it has anything to do with food or fun. This is Serena, after all."

Chapter 9
Love Raffle

It was free period. Homeroom teacher, Miss Patricia Haruna, had dismissed math class early so that she could make a lunch date. Most of the class was on the way to the cafeteria, but Serena hadn't moved from her desk. She hadn't budged all day, not since Molly had given her the flyer.

Molly sighed, scratching her head. "You look like some evil scientist removed your brain, Serena. If you had one to begin with."

Serena didn't move. "No, no, no," she chanted. "No, no, no..."

Melvin Grier popped up, in his usual gopher-like fashion. He cocked his head so that his

mars attacks

coke-bottle glasses gleamed. "What's up with Serena?" he asked in his high, squeaky voice. "Is that the new issue of Computer Stuff Monthly?"

Molly glanced over at Melvin skeptically. "C'mon, Melvin," she said flatly. "Do you really think Serena reads anything besides Sailor V?"

Melvin thought on that a moment. "Sushi Girl?" he asked.

Molly sighed. "It's a flyer for that new cruise line," she replied. "You know, Sunset Romance."

Serena moaned loudly, then began pounding her head on the desk.

"Serena!" Molly cried, grabbing her friend. "Cut it out! You're losing brain cells, and you don't have any to spare!"

Serena laid her head on Molly's shoulder. "But you said this thing's sold out," she complained. "Why'd you wait until today to show it to me, Molly? You should've given it to me a month ago. Then I could've booked tickets and gone with the man of my dreams!"

Melvin grinned happily and took her hands. "I'm honored you'd consider me!" he exclaimed.

"Oh, Serena, next time there's a cruise, I promise, we'll go together! We'll talk, and we'll dance, and we'll sit out on the deck at night and watch the sta--"

Serena held up a fist. "Wanna get pounded?"

Melvin lowered his head and released her. "No, ma'am."

Serena gazed sadly at the flyer. A young man and woman, holding hands and smiling, were standing on the deck of a gorgeous ship. SUNSET ROMANCE CRUISE, it read, THE PERFECT GET-AWAY FOR THE PERFECT COUPLE.

It looked so romantic, Serena thought with a sigh. It was the kind of thing she'd always dreamed about, going on a romantic getaway with a guy she was totally in love with. If only she had tickets, she'd get Andrew to go—then he'd have to fall in love with her for sure.

She could see his ocean-blue eyes. Ocean-blue?! Andrew didn't have ocean-blue eyes. That creep who always seemed to bump into her did! She shook her head violently to clear the image from her mind.

As if, she thought angrily. That creep was

the last person she'd want to go with. And she couldn't believe Raye had said he was good-looking. Being a jerk was totally unattractive.

"Don't be upset about missing the cruise, Serena," Melvin said. "It's an overnight trip where hardly anyone sleeps. We're junior-high school students, we shouldn't be up that late."

Serena and Molly glared at him. Melvin swallowed nervously.

"Don't be ridiculous," Molly snapped back. "Anyone would be willing to give up one night's sleep for the romance of a lifetime."

Serena rubbed her tired eyes. "What I wouldn't give for tickets to that cruise." She rested her head on her desk and closed her eyes.

Melvin frowned. "Then why don't you try to win tickets?" he asked. "They're raffling off the last four tickets at Crossroads Center."

Like a jack-in-the-box, Serena jumped out of her seat and tackled Melvin. Melvin squeaked as they went crashing to the floor.

"YOU'RE KIDDING!" Serena screamed as she grabbed his shoulders.

Melvin covered his face with his hands. "It's

true!" he said, his voice high and squeaky. "There's a raffle this afternoon!" He began to tremble. "Just please, Serena, don't kill me!"

Serena laughed with excitement and jumped up. "I don't wanna kill you," she cried, clapping her hands. "In fact, I almost wanna kiss you!"

"Really?" Melvin brightened.

"I said, 'almost.'" With that, Serena ran out the door, her ponytails blowing in the wind behind her.

There's still a chance, she thought. She still might be able to go on the cruise. "Oh, Andrew," she yelled, "you're gonna come sailing with me and we'll fall in love at last!"

As Serena disappeared down the hallway, Molly sat back down at her desk. She shrugged.

"Do you think Serena realizes that she's leaving school during fourth period?"

Melvin frowned. "I don't think she realizes much of anything right now."

Molly sighed and covered her face. "Great," she muttered. "Miss H is gonna be mad."

mars attacks

In the Negaverse, Jedite paced quietly in the shadows. He was nervous, small drops of sweat beaded on his forehead. He brushed them away with a gloved hand.

"So, the queen's finally fed up with your failures?" a voice asked from behind.

Jedite didn't even turn around. "Get lost, Tidas," he said lowly. "I'm thinking."

A slim woman materialized in a swirling column of water. She had light silver skin, short black hair, and small, cold white eyes. She snapped her fingers to make the water disappear.

"This may be your last chance to gather energy for Queen Beryl," Tidas said simply. "She's fed up with you. I'm one of her strongest servants, why don't you let me help you?"

"Because I don't need your help!" Jedite was furious. "I'm perfectly capable of gathering energy on my own!"

Tidas was quiet for a moment. "You're out of ideas," she said at last.

"I am not!"

"You're a good liar."

Jedite growled and turned to her. "Look," he

said darkly, "I don't have time for this. What do you want?"

Tidas brushed a strand of shining black hair from her eyes. "I have a plan," she replied. "A good one. One that could make Beryl happy and save your rear end."

Jedite narrowed his eyes. "I seriously doubt you could make a plan that's better than any of mine."

"We'll see about that." Tidas held up a small flyer. There was a couple pictured on the front, under the words: SUNSET ROMANCE CRUISES.

"I call it, 'The Romantic Cruise Strategy.'" Tidas' cold eyes glittered. "And it'll get us more energy than you could ever imagine."

Serena handed the man her money, closed her eyes and prayed. Please, she thought, let her win this time.

She reached into the box of paper slips and grabbed one. She pulled the slip out and quickly unfolded it.

Nothing.

"Noooo!" Serena cried, burying her face in

her hands.

The man behind the stall shook his head. "Sorry, miss," he said. "No luck. Perhaps next time. Would you like to try again?"

She had already tried ten times.

"I'm out of money," Serena answered sadly. "Otherwise, I'd be trying all day."

The man nodded. "Well then, thank you for playing. Have a good day."

Serena turned from the stall and walked away. Doomed, she thought. She would never get those tickets.

Her thoughts were broken as she crashed into Raye. Serena yelped and tumbled to the ground.

"Serena." Raye frowned as she helped the blonde up. "Why don't you watch where you're going?"

Serena sighed. "Sorry," she mumbled. "Wasn't thinking."

"You never think." Raye brushed off her skirt. She went to the T.A. Private School for Girls, and her school uniform—a dark skirt, gray jacket, and brick-red collar-bow—was much more sophisticated-looking than Serena's.

Raye looked at Serena. "What's wrong with you?" she asked as she shifted her book bag from one hand to the other. "You look down. Did the ice cream man outrun you today?"

"Cut it out, Raye." Serena glared at the priestess. "I just spent two weeks' allowance trying to win tickets to the Sunset Romance Cruise, and I lost every time."

"Sunset Romance Cruise?" Raye sighed. "You're such a pathetic romantic, Serena. Why bother trying to win tickets? You don't have anyone to go with."

"You are so mean, Raye!" Serena shouted. She clenched her fists. "Actually, there was somebody I was gonna ask, but since I didn't win the tickets, I'll never get to go with him." She thrust her chin in the air and gripped her backpack strap. "Now if you don't mind, I'm going to go home and sulk."

Raye stepped aside to let her pass. "Be my guest," she said as Serena stomped by.

The priestess watched as the blonde walked out of the mall. Raye paused a moment, then made a beeline for the raffle table.

Chapter 10
I Have To
Go With Who?

"Raye WON?!"

Amy covered her mouth. "Um," she whispered, "I wasn't supposed to tell you."

Serena stomped her foot angrily, almost crushing Luna.

"That hypocrite!" she cried. "I was doing that raffle for a solid hour yesterday, and she came by and said I was stupid for doing it. Then she goes and wins the thing on her first try?"

Amy looked to her neat brown loafers and shrugged. "Raye thought a cruise might be a good experience," she said simply. "She focused her priestess powers and was able to pick the winner out of the box."

"So she cheated!"

Amy frowned. "Well, considering she was using her inborn power, not really."

Serena slapped her forehead in frustration. She couldn't believe it. Raye was a hypocrite, and a sneak.

"As if that bossy priestess has anyone to go with," Serena said darkly. "She couldn't get a boy to go with her if she was the last female on Earth."

Amy looked up. "She's not going with a boy, Serena."

Serena's eyes narrowed. "So I suppose she's just going to throw away the other ticket? Not that I'd be surprised if she did."

"She's taking me."

Serena stopped dead in her tracks.

"WHAT?!" Serena gripped the blue-haired girl's shoulders. "She's taking you?! When she knows I want to go more than anything?!"

"I told her that repeatedly," Amy replied in her defense. "I told her you wanted to go, and that you tried so hard to win those tickets, but she said she wanted to go with me. We hardly get to talk because we go to different schools, and she wanted to discuss Sailor Scout strategies."

Serena scowled. Yeah, right, she thought. Raye just couldn't get a guy, so she decided to take Amy just to get Serena mad.

"Besides," Amy said, looking away. "I love the ocean. I'd like to see it under the stars."

Serena shook her fists angrily. "That's not the point of a romantic cruise!" she shouted. "You need a cute guy!"

Amy frowned.

"Look," Luna said from Serena's feet. It seemed the cat was at last ready to butt in. "I can't say what Raye did to get those tickets was very honest, but what's done is done. Enough complaining."

"What?" Serena glared down at the cat. "Don't you find this whole situation wrong, Luna?"

Luna rolled her eyes. "Serena, Amy and Raye have worked hard against the Enemy. They deserve a little break."

"But I wanted this more than anything!" Serena moaned. She buried her face in her hands. Raye was so cruel to her.

"Get over it," Luna said shortly. "And see them off tonight. They're your friends."

Serena looked up, eyes hard. "No." She shook her head. "No offense to you, Amy, but I'm not seeing you off. Raye doesn't deserve my blessing."

"I won't be offended," Amy murmured. "I can understand you're upset."

"Serena." Luna growled. "You are going to see them off tonight. It's the right thing to do."

Serena shook her head. "I am not, Luna." Raye wasn't going to get anything from Serena after denying her those tickets.

"Yes." Luna's eyes flashed. "You are."

Serena scowled. "No, I'm not!"

That night, Serena stood on the Crossroads Pier to see Raye, Amy, and the Sunset Romance Cruise off.

Serena crossed her arms. "Bossy cat," she muttered. Luna, who was perched on Serena's shoulder, ignored the insult.

The Sunset Romance Cruise Liner was a huge ship, decorated with bright lights and fancy furniture. A small orchestra played on deck while all the happy couples boarded.

Serena sighed. It was like watching the beginning of *Titanic*. The ship was so pretty and romantic—Serena wished it would sink.

Amy and Raye walked up the gangplank. The blue-haired girl spotted Serena and waved.

Serena waved back weakly. "Lucky Amy," she mumbled. "Though I don't know why she's even bothering without a guy."

"Everything is boys to you." Luna licked a paw as she spoke. "Amy and Raye can have lots of fun without boys."

Serena muttered angrily and shoved her hands into her windbreaker's pockets. Luna had an answer for everything. So Serena had guys on her mind all the time, what was wrong with that? Luna just did not understand.

"Well, well," drawled a voice from behind Serena. "Fancy seeing you here."

Serena recognized the voice—her heart froze in her chest. Like this night could get any worse, she thought as she slowly turned around.

The dark-haired young man smiled. "Don't

fall into the water. I'm willing to bet you can't swim."

Serena tried to come up with a snappy reply, but her mouth didn't seem to be working. The guy was dressed in a white dress shirt and black dress pants. His midnight hair fell over his forehead, and softly caught the silver moonlight. Serena hated to admit it, but he did look good.

Serena's heart was pounding so hard she could barely catch her breath. Standing there by the water, she could see that his eyes were one shade lighter than the ocean.

The young man cocked his head. "You OK?"

Serena suddenly realized she hadn't stopped staring. She coughed loudly as her cheeks burned. "I'm fine!" she snapped, whipping back around. She swallowed hard. "Or at least I was until you showed! Can't you ever leave me alone?"

He laughed. "But if I did that, I'd lose out on the fun of making you angry."

His laugh sent a shiver down her spine. She tried to ignore the smell of his Nautica cologne. "You're such a creep!" was all she could think to shoot back.

mars attacks

"Going on the cruise?"

Serena set her jaw. "No."

"Why not?"

"Who cares why not!" Serena didn't like the way her heart was thundering in her chest. She wanted him gone. "Just leave me alone. I'm not in the mood to deal with you right now!"

There was a moment of silence between them. The guy couldn't see her face with her back turned to him, but Serena was afraid he could hear her heavy breathing. Finally, Serena heard him take a step.

A warm hand took hers—Serena's heart froze. The guy's long fingers gently opened her hand, and placed a rigid piece of paper in her palm. He closed her fist over the paper.

"My luck yesterday was better than I thought," he said as he walked past her towards the ship. "I was hoping to find someone to take that ticket off my hands."

Serena could only stare as he walked to the gangplank and boarded the ship. When he had disappeared from view, she looked at her hand. She raised her fist and slowly opened it.

There, in her palm, was a ticket for the Sunset Romance Cruise. The words, SPECIAL RAFFLE WINNER, were written across the top in gold letters.

Serena's lips barely parted. "The raffle," she whispered. Four tickets had been raffled off. Raye had won two. Serena hadn't bothered to wonder who had won the others.

"Looks like some of his luck rubbed off on you," Luna commented from Serena's feet.

Serena suddenly snapped out of her daze. She shook her head to clear it.

The guy had given her a ticket. Why? They weren't a couple. Couple, Serena thought. Why did that word bother her so?

Serena looked to make sure he wasn't waiting for her. She was afraid that if she saw him again her heart would burst. And the scariest part of all was that she didn't know why.

The coast was clear. Serena grabbed the cat and ran up the gangplank just as the ship got underway.

Raye and Amy walked along the deck of the

ship and watched the pier get smaller in the distance. Amy leaned against the railing as the evening breeze caught her green velvet dress.

"The stars are so beautiful," she said. "What a gorgeous evening for a cruise."

Raye's bright scarlet dress fluttered about her knees. She crossed her arms over her chest and leaned back against the railing.

"Mmm," she agreed. "Beautiful."

Amy turned to the priestess. "Raye?" the blue-haired girl asked. "Is something wrong?"

Raye exhaled loudly. "Not really," she replied. "I'm just not used to doing nothing. I'm usually doing schoolwork or working at the temple, and now that I'm a Sailor Scout I have Sailor business, too." She looked up and gave a half-smile. "I'm usually running around, doing things all the time. It's a little strange to be on a boat where I can just stand around and relax."

Amy smiled. "Then enjoy it, Raye. This may be the nicest vacation you'll have for a while."

Raye tilted her head to the sky and breathed deeply. "Yeah," she whispered.

"Do you think Serena will be OK?"

Raye screwed up her face. "She'll be fine," she answered flatly. "That girl needs to get her head out of the clouds, anyway. Sailor Moon cannot be a pathetic romantic."

Amy frowned. "Don't you think you're a little rough on her?"

"I'm just trying to toughen her up, Amy."

Amy shook her head. "You underestimate her, Raye. Serena is pretty good in a fight."

Chapter 11
Captain Hottie

"You're lost."

Serena glared down at her cat. "I am not."

Luna narrowed her eyes. "Serena, admit it. You have no idea where we are."

Serena frowned and looked around her. She had been stuck wandering around the bowels of the ship for more than half an hour. When she had boarded, Serena had seen the guy again, and had ducked down a stairwell to avoid him. Now she was lost.

"I'm going in circles," Serena mumbled. "Oh, God, Luna, we're gonna be stuck in the belly of this boat forever."

Luna poked her head above Serena's embracing arms. "It's awfully quiet around here," the cat commented. "Rather odd, don't you think? I thought there was supposed to be a full crew manning this boat. We haven't bumped into a single person."

"It is a little odd," Serena admitted. "But before you go claiming that this is the work of the Enemy—"

Serena went quiet as the boiler room door opened, and a man in a captain's uniform walked out. Serena gulped and dove behind a bunch of crates.

"Serena," Luna whispered. "Why are you hiding?"

Serena turned red. "I'm embarrassed," she whispered back. She took another look at the captain. "I've been wandering around like an idiot. That captain's a hottie. The last thing I wanna do is look like an moron in front of a hottie."

Luna sighed. "Serena," the cat muttered as she watched the captain walk by, "sometimes you act like a complete—"

The cat stopped in mid-sentence and

pricked up her ears.

Serena saw that Luna's radar was up. "What's wrong, Luna?"

Luna's eyes narrowed as she looked at the captain. "Serena, look closer at that man," the cat ordered. "Doesn't he look familiar?"

Serena squinted. "No," she replied. "It's too dark down here to see him well." But Serena did notice that he was really cute. His golden hair fell in thick locks from under his captain's hat.

"Serena," Luna said quickly, "I'm getting major bad vibes from him."

Serena waved a hand. "You think everyone's the Enemy. You'd feel bad vibes from the Pillsbury Doughboy."

Luna scowled. "I'm serious, Serena, something is wrong here. This place is too quiet, and the captain is giving off an aura of evil energy."

Serena sighed and shook her head. As if such a babe could be evil. That captain was such a blond hottie.

Serena froze. Blond hottie?

"Oh great," she said with a moan, lowering her head. "Not again. Jedite."

"Exactly." Luna nodded gravely. "I'm quite sure that was him. Follow him."

Serena picked up her cat and slipped out from behind the crates.

"What is with that stupid dork?" Serena asked. "He's everywhere."

Another fun time ruined by Jedite, she thought to herself. He's such a pathetic loser. He knows he can't beat the Sailor Scouts, but still he keeps trying.

When the captain reached the engine room, he opened the door and stepped inside. He shut the door behind him. Serena heard the 'click' as the door locked.

Using all the stealth she had gained from her years of experience slipping downstairs for a midnight snack, Serena snuck over to the engine room door and peeked into its window. The captain was talking animatedly with a female crew member.

The captain took off his hat. Definitely Jedite, Serena thought—she'd know that adorable blond cowlick anywhere. She pressed her ear against the window and tried to make out the conversation.

"...tonight," the woman insisted. "The people...energy."

Jedite nodded. "Six hundred... dance..." He walked closer to the door. "...with all the crew unconscious, nobody can stop us."

Serena's eyes widened. "Oh my God," she whispered. "They're gonna suck up the energy of everyone on the ship!"

Luna looked up quickly. "Then that means..."

"No!" Serena slapped a hand over her mouth. "Amy and Raye!"

Amy placed her napkin on her lap and frowned. She stared at the steaks on her plate.

"What's wrong?" Raye asked from across the table. The priestess, too, only stared at her dinner.

Amy bit her lip. "Um, I don't know if the chef is, how should I put this, qualified for his job," she said hesitatingly. "These steaks are—"

"Inedible," Raye finished, jamming her fork into one of the meat slabs. She lifted it up, only to see the steak hang stiffly from her utensil. "You could make a handbag out of this thing."

"Indeed," Amy agreed, nudging a steak with her knife. She gave a half-smile. "Well, I wasn't very hungry, anyway."

Raye smirked. "Me neither."

"Ladies, gentleman!" said a slick voice on the intercom. "I hope everyone's enjoying dinner, because now it's time for the real romance to kick in."

Amy and Raye looked up.

"The Sunset Romance Twilight Extravaganza will be beginning shortly in the ballroom," the voice announced. "Please come with your partner. We'll be waiting!"

All the couples quickly stood up and headed for the ballroom. Raye sighed and pushed back in her chair.

"Great," she murmured as she rocked to her feet. "A dance. Another chance for us to watch young couples make kissy faces at each other."

Amy smiled slightly and shrugged. "It's all right," she responded as she stood up and took Raye's hand. "Don't let all the romance bother you. You came here to enjoy yourself, so let's have some fun."

Raye did not hear Amy—she had spotted something. A dark-haired young man, alone, slipped away from the crowd and disappeared around a corner.

"Raye?" Amy shook the girl slightly. "Are you all right?"

Raye shook her head to clear it. "Fine," she answered after a moment, looking down. She frowned. "Just thought I saw someone I know."

Amy and Raye tagged along behind the mob of happy couples. The ballroom was large and elegant. A huge skylight in the domed ceiling made it seem as if they were under the stars. A crescent moon glowed outside in the evening sky.

Raye's high heels clicked on the marble floor. Suddenly, she stopped and narrowed her eyes. Amy looked to her, puzzled.

"What's the matter, Raye?"

Raye's eyes flickered purple. "Evil," she whispered under her breath. "There's evil here."

Amy froze. As the rest of the cruise's passengers spread out on the dance floor, a large, crystal sphere lowered from the ceiling.

Amy took a step back, eyes wide. "You mean the Enemy?"

Before Raye could answer, Tidas and Jedite stepped onto the stage. Tidas wore her crew uniform; Jedite was in his captain's outfit. "Please," Tidas called, her lips curling into a smile. "Enjoy yourselves."

With that, the music started and the crystal sphere began to turn. Couples laughed and began dancing, twirling across the marble floor.

None of the dancers saw the white light that ebbed slowly from their bodies.

"Their energy," Raye whispered as she grabbed Amy's wrist, "that crystal sphere's absorbing it."

Amy sucked in a breath. "What will we do? We can't transform here," she said hurriedly. "The doors locked behind us. We won't be able to leave without making a scene, they'll know it's us—our true identities will be revealed."

"We have to do something."

Raye clenched her teeth and pulled Amy close as the couples around them started moaning and falling to the floor.

mars attacks

"So...weak." They groaned as the ball drew the white light out of them.

Jedite laughed. He clenched his fists and stared hungrily at the guests.

"Yes," he drawled. "Sacrifice all of your energy, fools. I won't be defeated this time."

Amy bit her lip as the guests collapsed to the floor around her. "Raye?" she asked desperately. "What are we going to do?"

Serena ran across the deck, panting. The ship was like a maze. Where was that stupid ballroom?

"You have to hurry!" Luna shouted as she ran beside Serena. Amy and Raye may have gotten caught in the trap!"

Serena swallowed hard and ran faster. Please, she thought as her sneakers pounded against the wooden deck. Please let Amy and Raye be all right! The dark-haired guy, too. She couldn't let the bad guys hurt him, no matter how much of a creep he could be. Serena flew around a corner and bit her lip so hard it bled.

Please, her mind screamed. "I'm coming!"

Chapter 12
Love Energy

"What?!" Jedite narrowed his eyes at the two girls standing in the ballroom. "Why hasn't your energy been drained?"

Couples lay in heaps on the floor all around Amy and Raye. The moonlight shining through the skylight bathed them in silver. The two girls glared but said nothing.

Tidas frowned.

"Our energy-absorbing sphere is designed to drain love energy," she said. "Those two didn't come with dates, so it didn't work on them."

Jedite snorted loudly. "What kind of losers come on a romantic cruise without dates?"

mars attacks

Raye scowled. "We're strong, independent women," she said. "We don't need dates to have fun."

Jedite raised an eyebrow. "That's a pretty lame excuse."

Raye's eyes flashed. "Well, you're a pretty lame excuse for a cook," she shot back. "Those steaks you served for dinner tasted like cardboard."

Tidas narrowed her eyes. "I cooked those steaks," she said darkly. "Anyone who insults my cooking will be destroyed!"

Raye flipped her midnight hair over her shoulder. "Looks like someone can't take criticism."

Tidas snarled. "Little brat!" she yelled as she shot out her hand. Her fingertips glowed blue. "Forget your energy. I'll just vaporize you!"

Amy reached into her dress pocket. "Enemy or not," she whispered, "we have no choice. Transform, Raye."

Raye nodded slightly and reached for her pocket. Suddenly, a familiar voice called out.

"Mind if I join the fun?"

Amy and Raye looked up, and smiled.

There, perched high on the balcony, was Sailor Moon. A small black cat with a crescent moon on its forehead stood by her side.

"Not you again!" Jedite called as he clenched his fists. "Stop bothering me and give up!"

Sailor Moon crossed her arms and smirked. "Gimme a break," she called back, her eyes bright and determined. "You're the one who should give up."

Serena saw that Amy and Raye were OK. Thank God, she thought, smiling.

Luna looked up at Serena. "Amy and Raye can't transform or the Enemy will discover their identities," she whispered. "You'll have to fight solo until they can sneak off."

Serena gulped. She'd have to fight Jedite and his lady partner all by herself.

Serena thrust her chin into the air. "Pure love is a beautiful thing," she announced. "For the sake of young love—and for the sake of all the cool, fashionable girls without guys who will eventually snag the hottest ones of all—you must be stopped!" Always nice adding a touch of real life to these speeches, she thought.

mars attacks

Serena pointed menacingly. "I am Sailor Moon, Champion of Justice and defender of the innocent, and on behalf of the moon, you're punished!"

Jedite growled. "This was your plan," he reminded Tidas as he stepped off the stage. "You deal with this."

Serena's eyes widened. "Hey!" she yelled. "Get back here! I haven't kicked your butt yet!"

Tidas shed her crew uniform, revealing a sleek silk fighting suit of blue and silver. Like a ninja, she jumped onto the balcony and smashed full force into Serena.

Serena yelped as she and the villain crashed through the glass. The Champion of Justice barely managed to tear free before slamming hard into the deck below.

Tidas stood slowly, her now-white eyes glittering dangerously. "You think you're strong?" She held up a fist; water began to swirl around it. "Let's see you defeat me."

Serena got to her feet and swallowed. Now would be a great time for my fellow Scouts appear, she thought hopefully. "OK, guys," she muttered to herself, "you can save me anytime now."

"Sailor Moon!" Luna called from the balcony. "Be strong! You can win!"

Easy for her to say, Serena thought. She wished she could watch from up there, where it was nice and safe.

Tidas threw out her palms out. A huge wave of water shot over the side of the boat and crashed into Serena. The Champion of Justice was washed across the deck as the rushing water surged over her head.

"Guggh!" Serena choked as she grabbed the railing and held on for dear life. When the water finally stopped rushing by, she gasped and reached for her tiara. "That water's freezing!" she whispered breathlessly.

Tidas' eyes narrowed. She flew forward, grabbing Serena's wrists and slamming the Champion of Justice into a wall. Stars burst in Serena's head.

"You're slow," Tidas murmured as Serena fought to catch her breath. "How do you really expect to defeat Jedite if you can't defeat me?" The woman lowered her head, her breath cold on Serena's face.

Serena screwed up her face. "Gross! Don't breathe on me. Ever heard of Certs?"

Tidas snarled and raised a fist. "I've had it with you!" She roared.

"MERCURY BUBBLES BLAST!"

Thick, stifling bubbles suddenly clogged the air. Tidas coughed and stumbled back, letting go of Serena.

"MARS FIRE IGNITE!"

Fire ripped through the deck and slammed into Tidas. The woman screamed as scarlet and orange flames engulfed her body.

"Don't you touch our Sailor Moon!" Sailor Mars shouted.

Serena smiled in relief and pulled her tiara from her head. She aimed for Tidas. That lady wasn't so scary when she was trapped in Raye's fire, Serena thought. It was so much easier to be brave when she had back up.

"We'll never be beaten by you stupid villains," Serena called. "We're a team, lady. We fight as one, and that's why we never lose."

Serena threw the tiara with all her strength. "MOON TIARA ACTION!"

Tidas screamed as a golden light rushed through her body. The light exploded, and Tidas burst into flames. The fire quickly extinguished itself, as the dusty remains sprinkled to the wooden deck.

"Another villain dusted!" Serena exclaimed.

An angry cry came from behind Serena. She spun around to see a furious Jedite, his fists clenched and his eyes burning.

"You stupid brats!" he screamed. "I'm sick of you ruining my plans! I'll destroy you once and for all!"

Serena scowled. "That's what every bad guy says," she said, not impressed. "And every bad guy we've gone against has ended up as a pile of dust."

Jedite's eyes flared with a blue fire. "I am not a petty servant," he said with a hiss, raising a hand above his head. "I'll be back. And the next time, I won't play around!"

Jedite snapped his fingers, and a black portal appeared behind him. He stepped into it and disappeared.

Serena laughed.

"Well." She grinned. "Guess we don't have to fight him after all. That Jedite is really a wuss."

Amy stared at where the portal had been; she gripped her chin in thought. "He doesn't seem to fear us," she said finally. "Why didn't he stay and fight?"

"Probably so he can get the upper hand."

Amy and Serena turned to Raye. The priestess was staring off into the evening sky. "What?" Serena asked.

"Think about it," Raye answered. "There's three of us and one of him. He probably retreated so he can fight us later, on his own terms."

"His own terms?" Amy touched her lips. "Oh, God. You don't think he'll take hostages, do you?"

Raye shrugged. "God knows."

Serena's eyes widened. Hostages? This could be bad. As if that creep Jedite hadn't done enough to the poor people of Crossroads. She didn't want to think about what he might be planning for their next fight.

"Whatever he does," Luna said, walking up

to them, "you'll all have to be ready. Jedite seems determined to stop you for good. The next time you face him, it will be a fight to the finish." The cat focused orange-red eyes on the girls. "Be prepared for it."

"Right." Amy nodded. "We'll be ready."

Raye turned back to the sea. "His abuse has gone on long enough."

Serena let her fingers play with her skirt as she stared at the wooden deck. A final fight. She had teased Jedite about being a loser before, but after seeing the blue fire in his eyes, she knew not to underestimate him again.

The muffled sound of footsteps made Serena look up in time to see a shadowy figure disappear around a corner. Serena ran to the corner to see who was there, but saw nothing.

"That's weird," she murmured. "If everybody on this ship is passed out—"

A glimmer of red in the darkness made her stop dead. Serena walked over to it.

A single red rose lay on the wooden deck.

Serena fell to her knees. Carefully, she picked up the flower, staring at it with wide eyes.

Her fingers curled gently around the petals. She gazed up.

"Tuxedo Mask?" she whispered under her breath.

But there was no one there. Serena sat alone in the darkness.

The black portal brought Jedite to Queen Beryl's throne room. As soon as he stepped out of the vortex, he dropped to one knee and lowered his head. "My queen."

"Jedite." Queen Beryl's voice was very cold. "Why did you come back?"

"Queen Beryl," Jedite began, "allow me to explain. I have decided to fight the Sailor Scouts as soon as I can set up a place to have a proper battl--"

CRACK

Jedite fell to the floor, stunned. Queen Beryl had unleashed a lightning bolt from her crystal ball. Jedite's clothes sizzled, and a trail of blood ran down his cheek.

"Tidas was one of my best servants!" Beryl roared, jumping to her feet. The dark air trembled around her. "You not only let her be defeated, you failed to get me any energy, and you failed to get rid of those Sailor Scouts!"

Jedite's eyes widened. He crawled to his knees. "Please," he said, clasping his hands together. "Queen Beryl, I assure you that I--"

Another bolt of lightning shot from the crystal, slamming Jedite into a pillar. He let out a gurgling cry as he slid to the floor.

Beryl held up her hand, her nails glittering. "I'm through with you, general!" she yelled. "Your failures end here!"

Jedite started to shake. His eyes filled with dread. "But, Queen Beryl--"

"Silence!" Beryl grabbed her floating crystal ball and snapped her fingers. Red lightning crackled inside the crystal ball.

Beryl's orange eyes blazed. " You have one more chance. Fail me again, and I'll destroy you!"

The Sunset Romance Cruise ship floated quietly in the water. The fight had ruined much of the deck.

Serena stood at the railing, clutching the red rose close to her chest. Her golden hair danced in the gusting, evening wind.

Had Tuxedo Mask really come? She hadn't been able to see the stranger, but all the passengers on the boat had been unconscious. Whoever it was, she thought, couldn't have been a guest. But if it really had been him, how had he known there would be trouble onboard? And how had he gotten to a ship way out at sea?

Serena bit her lip.

"Hey," a voice called. "Haven't puked from sea sickness yet, I see."

Serena's breath caught in her throat. The dark-haired young man who had given her the ticket walked up beside her and rested his arms on the railing.

"Are you OK?" she whispered.

The young man's eyes widened. "Yeah," he answered slowly. "Why wouldn't I be?"

Serena realized the passengers had probably thought the attack had been a dream. She turned red and looked away.

"I just mean, lots of people get seasick," she mumbled. "I though you might, too."

"Is that concern I hear?" The guy smiled. He

clicked his tongue. "Never thought a word of kindness would pass through your lips, blondie."

Serena looked up at him. She tried to read his expression.

"Where'd you get the rose?" he asked.

Serena nearly dropped it. "I found it."

"Ah." The young man looked out at sea. "Sure it was meant for you?"

Serena gave a start. She hadn't considered that. Not meant for her?

A moment of shocked silence passed between them before he turned back to her. He saw her expression, and a smile curled his lips.

"You look shocked, blondie."

Serena struggled to get her voice to work. Why was her heart pounding so madly now that he was close to her?

"I... I..."

She could feel her cheeks turning pink again. She turned her head away.

"I was hoping it was," she murmured at last.

Serena heard the railing creak as the guy shifted his arms. A warm finger touched her cheek. "Hey," he said.

mars attacks

Serena's heart stopped as the guy's fingers held her chin. Slowly, he turned her face to his.

The moonlight reflected off his ocean-blue eyes. He smiled. "Well," he said softly, "maybe it was meant for you, after all."

Serena couldn't breathe. He released her and turned away. "Anyway," he said, "catch ya later. Don't trip and fall off the boat, OK?" He walked off down the deck and disappeared around a corner.

It seemed like hours before Serena's heart started beating again. She slowly reached up and felt her chin. The spot where he had touched her was still warm.

What was wrong with her? Why was she like this around him? He could be such creep when he made fun of her. She had yelled at him time and time again for being so mean. Had something changed between them? And why had her mind gone blank when he touched her?

Serena's hands closed tightly around the rose as she held it to her chest. She didn't know what was going on, but she knew he was scared of the way the guy made her feel. Something hurt deep inside whenever she looked into his ocean-blue eyes.

END

About the Writer

Lianne Sentar began her career as a writer at just 13 years-old working on an extensive fantasy novel entitled *Thief*. During the next two years, Ms. Sentar wrote hundreds of pages of fan-fiction and published them both on her website (http://members.tripod.com/~Lianne_Sentar/) as well as on other international fan-fic sites. Based on her initial online publishing success, Ms. Sentar self-published her first novella *Rain* in the fall of 1998. Since its initial release, *Rain* has been through four reprints and continues to grow in popularity. In the summer of 1999, 17-year-old Lianne began writing the *Sailor Moon* novel adaptations with the second *Sailor Moon* novel, *The Power of Love*. Ms. Sentar is currently working on her second original novel, the fantasy *Children of the Sky*. Ms. Sentar lives with her family in Connecticut, USA.